family
stir-fries

THE AUSTRALIAN
Women's Weekly

CONTENTS

AUSTRALIAN CUP AND SPOON MEASUREMENTS ARE METRIC. A CONVERSION CHART APPEARS ON PAGE 77.

We love stir-fries – especially in summer when we don't want to be spending time in a hot kitchen. This book is full of recipes for simple and fast stir-fries – nutritious food that's on the table with a minimum of fuss. And, what's more, they've all got the tick of approval from the family.

Pamela Clark

Food Director

FISH WITH MIXED VEGETABLES

prep + cook time 25 minutes serves 4
nutritional count per serving 15.1g total fat
(3g saturated fat); 1388kJ (332 cal);
12.9g carbohydrate; 32.4g protein; 6.7g fibre

2 cloves garlic, chopped finely
2½ tablespoons peanut oil
500g firm white fish fillets, cut into
    3cm pieces
350g broccolini, cut into 3cm lengths
1 large carrot (180g), cut into matchsticks
150g baby corn, halved lengthways
¼ cup (60ml) oyster sauce
1 tablespoon japanese soy sauce
1 tablespoon water

1 Combine garlic, 2 tablespoons of the oil and
fish in medium bowl. Heat wok; stir-fry fish, in
batches, until browned. Remove from wok.
2 Heat remaining oil in wok; stir-fry broccolini,
carrot and corn until vegetables are tender.
3 Return fish to wok with sauces and the
water; stir-fry until hot, season to taste.
Serve with steamed jasmine rice.
note We used blue-eye fillets in this recipe, but you
can use any firm white fish fillets.

SEAFOOD

honey prawns with pineapple

HONEY PRAWNS WITH PINEAPPLE

prep + cook time **30 minutes** serves **4**
nutritional count per serving **2g total fat**
(0.3g saturated fat); **807kJ (193 cal);**
16.7g carbohydrate; 24.3g protein; 4g fibre

800g uncooked medium king prawns
1 teaspoon peanut oil
1 large red capsicum (350g),
   chopped coarsely
150g snow peas, trimmed
2 cloves garlic, crushed
½ small pineapple (450g), chopped coarsely
230g can bamboo shoots, rinsed, drained
2 tablespoons tamarind concentrate
2 tablespoons kecap manis
1 tablespoon honey

1 Shell and devein prawns leaving tails intact.
2 Heat oil in wok; stir-fry prawns, capsicum,
peas and garlic until prawns change colour.
Add remaining ingredients; stir-fry until hot,
season to taste.
Serve with **steamed jasmine rice.**

PRAWNS WITH CRISPY THAI BASIL

prep + cook time **35 minutes** serves **4**
nutritional count per serving **6.3g total fat**
(0.8g saturated fat); 986kJ (236 cal);
10.5g carbohydrate; 31g protein; 6.1g fibre

1kg uncooked medium king prawns
vegetable oil, for shallow-frying
¼ cup loosely packed thai basil leaves
250g cherry tomatoes, halved
1 fresh long red chilli, chopped finely
¼ cup (60ml) sweet chilli sauce
2 tablespoons water
1 tablespoon brown sugar
350g broccolini, cut into 3cm lengths
1 medium red onion (170g), sliced thinly

1 Shell and devein prawns leaving tails intact.
2 Heat oil in wok; shallow-fry basil leaves, in
batches, until crisp. Drain on absorbent paper.
Discard oil, or save for another use.
3 Reheat wok; stir-fry tomato, chilli, sauce,
the water and sugar about 8 minutes or until
mixture is thickened slightly. Add prawns,
broccolini and onion to wok; stir-fry until
prawns change colour, season to taste. Serve
stir-fry topped with crisp basil leaves.

prawns with crispy thai basil

mussels in black bean sauce

MUSSELS IN BLACK BEAN SAUCE

prep + cook time **20 minutes** serves **4**
nutritional count per serving **8.4g total fat**
(1g saturated fat); 882kJ (211 cal);
9.4g carbohydrate; 23.2g protein; 2.1g fibre

2kg medium black mussels
1 tablespoon peanut oil
6cm piece fresh ginger (30g), sliced thinly
4 cloves garlic, sliced thinly
8 green onions, sliced thinly
4 fresh small red thai chillies, chopped finely
⅓ cup (100g) black bean sauce
¼ cup (60ml) fish stock
¼ cup (60ml) water
1 cup firmly packed fresh coriander leaves

1 Scrub mussels under cold water;
remove beards.
2 Heat oil in wok; stir-fry ginger, garlic, onion
and chilli until fragrant. Add sauce, stock and
the water; bring to the boil.
3 Add mussels; simmer, covered, about
5 minutes or until mussels open (discard any
that do not). Remove from heat; season to
taste, sprinkle with coriander.

NASI GORENG COMBO

prep + cook time **35 minutes** serves **4**
nutritional count per serving **15.2g total fat**
(3.7g saturated fat); 1822kJ (436 cal);
36.1g carbohydrate; 36.9g protein; 2.8g fibre

600g uncooked medium king prawns
1 teaspoon sesame oil
1 tablespoon peanut oil
1 medium brown onion (150g),
    chopped finely
3 cloves garlic, crushed
5cm piece fresh ginger (25g), grated
1 tablespoon sambal oelek
2 chicken thigh fillets (200g), cut into
    2cm pieces
3 cups (450g) cold cooked white long-grain
    rice (see note)
2 cups (160g) finely shredded wombok
1 cup (80g) bean sprouts

nasi goreng combo

4 green onions, sliced thinly
1 tablespoon kecap manis
4 eggs

1 Shell and devein prawns; chop coarsely.
2 Heat sesame oil with half the peanut oil in
wok; stir-fry onion, garlic, ginger and sambal
until onion softens. Add chicken; stir-fry until
browned. Add prawns; stir-fry until prawns
change colour. Add rice, wombok, sprouts,
onion and kecap manis; stir-fry until hot,
season to taste.
3 Meanwhile, heat remaining peanut oil in large
frying pan; fry eggs until barely set.
4 Serve nasi goreng topped with eggs.

note You need to cook 1½ cups (300g) white long-grain
rice the night before making this recipe. Spread it evenly
onto a tray and refrigerate overnight.

fish with kaffir lime and sugar snap peas

simmer, uncovered, until sauce thickens slightly.
3 Add peas, asparagus and the remaining
water; stir-fry until vegetables are tender.
Return fish to wok; stir-fry until hot, season
to taste.
4 Serve stir-fry sprinkled with lime leaves;
drizzle with lemon juice.
Serve with **steamed jasmine rice.**
note We used **blue-eye fillets in this recipe, but you
can use any firm white fish fillets.**

TUNA WITH FRIED NOODLES AND CABBAGE

prep + cook time **30 minutes** serves **4**
nutritional count per serving **19.7g total fat**
(5.7g saturated fat); 2220kJ (531 cal);
39.7g carbohydrate; 45.7g protein; 4.7g fibre

600g piece tuna, cut into 2cm pieces
¼ cup (60ml) light soy sauce
1 tablespoon wasabi
1 tablespoon lime juice
1 tablespoon grated palm sugar
440g fresh thin egg noodles
2 tablespoons peanut oil
1½ cups (120g) finely shredded cabbage
½ cup (125ml) sweet chilli sauce
1 tablespoon fish sauce
2 green onions, sliced thinly

1 Combine tuna, soy, wasabi, juice and
sugar in medium bowl. Drain tuna; reserve
2 tablespoons of the marinade.
2 Place noodles in large heatproof bowl, cover
with boiling water; separate with fork, drain.
3 Heat half the oil in wok; stir-fry tuna, in
batches, until browned and cooked as desired.
Remove from wok.
4 Heat remaining oil in wok; stir-fry cabbage
until wilted. Add noodles, reserved marinade,
sweet chilli sauce and fish sauce; stir-fry until
mixture boils, season to taste. Serve noodles
topped with tuna and onions.
note Salmon or ocean trout can be used in place
of the tuna.

FISH WITH KAFFIR LIME AND SUGAR SNAP PEAS

prep + cook time **20 minutes** serves **4**
nutritional count per serving **12.1g total fat**
(2.5g saturated fat); 1158kJ (277 cal);
11.2g carbohydrate; 29.5g protein; 3g fibre

2 tablespoons peanut oil
500g firm white fish fillets, cut into
    3cm pieces
1 medium brown onion (150g), sliced thinly
1 clove garlic, crushed
10cm stick fresh lemon grass (20g),
    chopped finely
1½ tablespoons brown sugar
½ cup (125ml) water
300g sugar snap peas, trimmed
170g asparagus, trimmed, cut into
    3cm lengths
2 fresh kaffir lime leaves, shredded finely
2 tablespoons lemon juice

1 Heat half the oil in wok; stir-fry fish, in
batches, until browned. Remove from wok.
2 Heat remaining oil in wok; stir-fry onion,
garlic and lemon grass until onion softens. Add
sugar and half the water; bring to the boil, then

tuna with fried noodles and cabbage

honeyed prawns

HONEYED PRAWNS

prep + cook time **35 minutes** serves **4**
nutritional count per serving **19.1g total fat**
(2.7g saturated fat); 2282kJ (546 cal);
61.6g carbohydrate; 31.9g protein; 1.8g fibre

1kg uncooked medium king prawns
1 cup (150g) self-raising flour
1¼ cups (310ml) water
1 egg
⅓ cup (50g) cornflour
vegetable oil, for deep-frying
⅓ cup (120g) honey
1 tablespoon toasted sesame seeds
2 green onions, sliced thinly

1 Shell and devein prawns leaving tails intact.
2 Sift flour into medium bowl; gradually whisk in the water and egg until batter is smooth. Toss prawns in cornflour; shake off excess. Dip prawns in batter, one at a time, without coating the tails; shake off excess.
3 Heat vegetable oil in wok; deep-fry prawns, in batches, until browned lightly. Drain on absorbent paper.
4 Meanwhile, place honey in small saucepan; bring to the boil. Remove from heat.
5 Divide prawns between serving bowls; drizzle with honey, sprinkle with seeds and green onions.

spiced coconut prawns

SPICED COCONUT PRAWNS

prep + cook time **20 minutes** serves **4**
nutritional count per serving **8.7g total fat**
(6.5g saturated fat); 1225kJ (293 cal);
11.9g carbohydrate; 38.5g protein; 6g fibre

1.25kg uncooked medium king prawns
500g cauliflower, cut into florets
200g broccoli, cut into florets
1 medium brown onion (150g), sliced thinly
2 cloves garlic, sliced thinly
2 fresh long red chillies, sliced thinly
1 teaspoon ground turmeric
2 teaspoons yellow mustard seeds
¼ teaspoon ground cardamom
½ teaspoon ground cumin
140ml can coconut milk
2 tablespoons mango chutney

1 Shell and devein prawns leaving tails intact. Combine prawns and remaining ingredients in large bowl.
2 Stir-fry ingredients in heated oiled wok until vegetables are just tender, season to taste.
Serve with **steamed jasmine rice.**

lemon, chilli and herb squid

LEMON, CHILLI AND HERB SQUID

prep + cook time 30 minutes serves 4
nutritional count per serving 15.6g total fat
(2.5g saturated fat); 1058kJ (253 cal);
1.7g carbohydrate; 25.7g protein; 1g fibre

600g cleaned squid hoods
2 cloves garlic, crushed
1 tablespoon chermoula spice mix
1 teaspoon finely grated lemon rind
2 tablespoons olive oil
100g baby asian greens
½ cup firmly packed fresh mint leaves
½ cup firmly packed fresh coriander leaves
lemon dressing
¼ cup (60ml) lemon juice
1 tablespoon olive oil
½ teaspoon caster sugar

1 Make lemon dressing.
2 Cut squid down centre to open out; score
inside in diagonal pattern, then cut squid into
3cm strips. Combine squid, garlic, spice mix,
rind and half the oil in medium bowl.
3 Heat remaining oil in wok; stir-fry squid, in
batches, until tender. Remove from wok.
4 Divide asian greens, herbs and squid between
serving plates; drizzle with lemon dressing.
lemon dressing Combine ingredients in
screw-top jar; shake well, season to taste.

GARLIC SEAFOOD

prep + cook time 40 minutes serves 4
nutritional count per serving 16.2g total fat
(3.1g saturated fat); 1509kJ (361 cal);
1.6g carbohydrate; 50.3g protein; 3.7g fibre

1kg uncooked medium king prawns
500g cleaned baby squid hoods
¼ cup (60ml) peanut oil
1 tablespoon finely chopped coriander root
   and stem mixture
2 fresh small red thai chillies
½ teaspoon coarsely ground black pepper
4 cloves garlic, crushed
170g asparagus, trimmed, chopped coarsely
175g broccolini, chopped coarsely
1 cup (80g) bean sprouts

garlic seafood

2 green onions, sliced thinly
2 tablespoons coarsely chopped
   fresh coriander
1 lime, cut into wedges

1 Shell and devein prawns leaving tails intact.
2 Cut squid down centre to open out; score
inside in diagonal pattern, then cut squid into
thick strips.
3 Heat half the oil in wok; cook seafood, in
batches, until prawns change colour. Remove
from wok.
4 Heat remaining oil in wok; stir-fry coriander
mixture, chilli, pepper and garlic until fragrant.
Add asparagus and broccolini; cook, stirring,
until vegetables are tender. Return seafood
to wok with sprouts; stir-fry until hot, season
to taste.
5 Serve stir-fry sprinkled with green onion and
coriander; accompany with lime.
note Buy coriander stems that have the root attached
for this recipe; wash well before using.

CHILLI PRAWNS WITH VERMICELLI

prep + cook time **25 minutes** serves **4**
nutritional count per serving **9.9g total fat**
(1.4g saturated fat); 1308kJ (313 cal);
21.3g carbohydrate; 29.7g protein; 9.4g fibre

Shell and devein 1kg uncooked medium king
prawns leaving heads and tails intact. Combine
prawns with ¼ cup sambal oelek in large bowl.
Place 190g rice vermicelli in medium heatproof
bowl, cover with boiling water; stand until
tender, drain. Heat oiled wok; stir-fry prawns, in
batches, until changed in colour. Remove from
wok. Reheat oiled wok; stir-fry 420g packet
1-minute stir-fry vegetable mix, 2 thinly sliced
fresh long red chillies and 2 tablespoons
massaman curry paste until vegetables soften.
Return half the prawns to wok with noodles;
stir-fry until hot, season to taste. Serve noodles
topped with remaining prawns.

PEPPERED TUNA WITH COLESLAW

prep + cook time **25 minutes** serves **4**
nutritional count per serving **18.7g total fat**
(5.8g saturated fat); 1597kJ (382 cal);
9.7g carbohydrate; 41.7g protein; 4.6g fibre

Coarsely chop 4 x 150g tuna steaks; combine
tuna with 1 tablespoon each sweet paprika and
coarsely cracked black pepper in medium
bowl. Cook tuna, in batches, in heated oiled
wok until cooked as desired, remove from wok.
Reheat oiled wok; stir-fry 450g packet coleslaw
mix and 2 tablespoons mee goreng paste until
vegetables wilt, season to taste. Serve topped
with tuna and 100g crisp fried noodles.

FAST SEAFOOD

CARAMEL FISH WITH PAK CHOY

prep + cook time **25 minutes** serves **4**
nutritional count per serving **12.5g total fat**
(2.5g saturated fat); 1676kJ (401 cal);
41.8g carbohydrate; 30.2g protein; 3.8g fibre

Heat ⅔ cup caster sugar in medium saucepan
over medium heat until sugar melts and turns
a light caramel colour. Remove pan from heat;
carefully add ⅓ cup fish sauce (liquid may spit).
Return pan to heat; simmer caramel sauce,
stirring, until sauce becomes syrupy; stir in
4 thinly sliced shallots. Boil, steam or microwave
1kg baby pak choy until just wilted; drain.
Meanwhile, cut 500g white fish fillets into 3cm
pieces. Heat 2 tablespoons peanut oil in wok;
stir-fry fish, in batches, until browned. Add
sauce; bring to the boil. Simmer, uncovered,
until fish is cooked. Divide pak choy between
serving plates; top with fish, drizzle with sauce.
Serve with **steamed jasmine rice.**

SATAY PRAWNS

prep + cook time **30 minutes** serves **4**
nutritional count per serving **18.1g total fat**
(4.4g saturated fat); 1672kJ (400 cal);
13.7g carbohydrate; 43.9g protein; 3.1g fibre

Shell and devein 1.5kg uncooked large king
prawns leaving tails intact. Thickly slice 1 large
red capsicum. Heat 1 tablespoon peanut oil in
wok; stir-fry prawns and capsicum until prawns
change colour. Add 250ml can satay sauce
and 3 thinly sliced green onions; stir-fry until
hot, season to taste.

SESAME CHICKEN

prep + cook time 40 minutes serves 4
nutritional count per serving 9.3g total fat
(1.6g saturated fat); 1325kJ (317 cal);
23.9g carbohydrate; 31.3g protein; 5.6g fibre

350g bean thread vermicelli
1 tablespoon peanut oil
2 chicken breast fillets (400g), sliced thinly
1 medium brown onion (150g), sliced thinly
1 clove garlic, crushed
300g broccolini, chopped coarsely
2 tablespoons fish sauce
1 tablespoon hot chilli sauce
2 tablespoons dark soy sauce
1 tablespoon toasted sesame seeds
1 fresh long red chilli, chopped finely
4 green onions, sliced thinly
1 cup (80g) bean sprouts

1 Place vermicelli in medium heatproof
bowl, cover with boiling water; stand until
just tender, drain.
2 Meanwhile, heat half the oil in wok; stir-fry
chicken, in batches, until browned. Remove
from wok.
3 Heat remaining oil in wok; stir-fry brown
onion, garlic and broccolini until onion softens.
4 Return chicken to wok with vermicelli,
combined sauces, sesame seeds and half the
chilli, half the green onion and half the sprouts;
stir-fry until hot, season to taste.
5 Serve stir-fry topped with remaining chilli,
green onion and sprouts.

3 Heat 2 teaspoons of the remaining oil in wok; stir-fry chicken, in batches, until browned. Remove from wok.

4 Heat remaining oil in wok; stir-fry brown onion and garlic until onion softens. Return chicken to wok with noodles, juice, sauce and sugar; stir-fry until hot. Remove from heat; stir in sprouts, green onion and half the coriander, season to taste.

5 Serve noodles topped with omelette, nuts and remaining coriander.

LEMON CHICKEN WITH ASIAN GREENS

prep + cook time **25 minutes** serves **4**
nutritional count per serving **15.6g total fat**
(3.5g saturated fat); 1162kJ (278 cal);
3.3g carbohydrate; 27.7g protein; 6.2g fibre

2 tablespoons peanut oil
500g chicken thigh fillets, sliced thinly
10cm stick fresh lemon grass (20g),
   chopped finely
3 cloves garlic, crushed
600g gai lan, trimmed, cut into 5cm lengths
1 small yellow capsicum (150g), sliced thinly
2 tablespoons lemon juice
2 tablespoons light soy sauce

1 Heat half the oil in wok; stir-fry chicken, in batches, until browned. Remove from wok.

2 Heat remaining oil in wok; stir-fry lemon grass and garlic until fragrant. Add gai lan, capsicum, juice and sauce; stir-fry until vegetables are tender.

3 Return chicken to wok; stir-fry until hot, season to taste.

Serve with steamed jasmine rice.

chicken pad thai

CHICKEN PAD THAI

prep + cook time **25 minutes** serves **4**
nutritional count per serving **14.3g total fat**
(2.9g saturated fat); 1789kJ (428 cal);
34.1g carbohydrate; 38.6g protein; 3g fibre

500g fresh wide rice noodles
1 tablespoon peanut oil
2 eggs, beaten lightly
500g chicken breast fillets, sliced thinly
1 medium brown onion (150g), sliced thinly
3 cloves garlic, crushed
2 tablespoons lime juice
2 tablespoons fish sauce
1 tablespoon brown sugar
1 cup (80g) bean sprouts
3 green onions, sliced thinly
½ cup coarsely chopped fresh coriander
¼ cup (35g) roasted unsalted peanuts,
   chopped coarsely

1 Place noodles in large heatproof bowl, cover with boiling water; separate with fork, drain.

2 Heat 1 teaspoon of the oil in wok. Pour egg into wok; cook omelette, tilting wok, until omelette is set. Remove omelette from wok; roll tightly then slice thinly.

lemon chicken with asian greens

chicken fried rice

CHICKEN FRIED RICE

prep + cook time **25 minutes** serves **4**
nutritional count per serving 21.9g total fat
(5.9g saturated fat); 2362kJ (565 cal);
52.6g carbohydrate; 37.2g protein; 3.8g fibre

1 tablespoon vegetable oil
2 eggs, beaten lightly
3 rindless bacon rashers (195g),
    chopped coarsely
2 cloves garlic, crushed
2cm piece fresh ginger (10g), grated
1½ cups (240g) coarsely chopped
    barbecued chicken
4 cups cold cooked white long-grain rice
    (see note)
1 cup (140g) frozen pea and corn mixture
¼ cup (60ml) light soy sauce
1 cup (80g) bean sprouts
6 green onions, sliced thinly

1 Heat half the oil in wok. Pour egg into wok;
cook omelette, tilting wok, until omelette is set.
Remove omelette from wok; roll tightly then
slice thinly.
2 Heat remaining oil in wok; stir-fry bacon,
garlic and ginger until bacon is crisp.
3 Add chicken; stir-fry 1 minute. Add rice, frozen
vegetables and sauce; stir-fry until hot. Add
sprouts, onion and omelette; stir-fry 1 minute,
season to taste.

notes You need to cook 2 cups (400g) of white
long-grain rice the day before making this recipe.
Spread evenly onto a tray; refrigerate overnight.
You need to purchase half a barbecued chicken
for enough chopped meat for this recipe.

almond and chilli chicken

ALMOND AND CHILLI CHICKEN

prep + cook time **30 minutes** serves **4**
nutritional count per serving 18.2g total fat
(2.3g saturated fat); 1417kJ (339 cal);
3.1g carbohydrate; 38.2g protein; 2.3g fibre

1 tablespoon peanut oil
½ cup (80g) blanched almonds
600g chicken breast fillets, sliced thinly
2 cloves garlic, crushed
2cm piece fresh ginger (10g), grated
2 teaspoons sambal oelek
1 tablespoon oyster sauce
1 tablespoon salt-reduced soy sauce
1 tablespoon dry sherry
6 green onions, cut into 3cm lengths

1 Heat 1 teaspoon of the oil in wok; stir-fry
nuts until browned lightly. Remove from wok.
2 Heat remaining oil in wok; stir-fry chicken, in
batches, until browned. Remove from wok.
3 Add garlic, ginger and sambal to wok; stir-fry
until fragrant. Return nuts and chicken to wok
with sauces and sherry; stir-fry until hot. Add
onion; stir-fry until combined, season to taste.
Serve with steamed jasmine rice.

chicken with mixed vegies and almonds

garlic until onion softens. Add broccolini, corn
and peas; stir-fry until vegetables are tender.
4 Return chicken to wok with nuts and sauces;
stir-fry until hot, season to taste. Serve with rice.

CHICKEN SINGAPORE NOODLES

prep + cook time **15 minutes** serves **4**
nutritional count per serving 15.5g total fat
(4.6g saturated fat); 1944kJ (465 cal);
32.7g carbohydrate; 41.9g protein; 3.2g fibre

450g fresh singapore noodles
1 teaspoon peanut oil
1 small brown onion (80g), sliced thinly
2 rindless bacon rashers (130g),
    chopped finely
3cm piece fresh ginger (15g), grated
1 tablespoon mild curry powder
3 cups (480g) shredded barbecued chicken
6 green onions, sliced thinly
1½ tablespoons light soy sauce
⅓ cup (80ml) sweet sherry

1 Place noodles in large heatproof bowl, cover
with boiling water; separate with fork, drain.
2 Heat oil in wok; stir-fry brown onion, bacon
and ginger until onion softens and bacon is
crisp. Add curry powder; stir-fry until fragrant.
3 Add noodles and remaining ingredients;
stir-fry until hot, season to taste.
note You need to purchase a large barbecued chicken
weighing approximately 900g to get the amount of
shredded meat needed for this recipe.

CHICKEN WITH MIXED VEGIES
AND ALMONDS

prep + cook time **35 minutes** serves **4**
nutritional count per serving 20.2g total fat
(3.1g saturated fat); 3515kJ (841 cal);
109.4g carbohydrate; 50.5g protein; 7.5g fibre

2½ cups (500g) jasmine rice
2 tablespoons peanut oil
600g chicken breast fillets, sliced thinly
1 medium brown onion (150g), sliced thinly
2 cloves garlic, crushed
350g broccolini, trimmed, chopped coarsely
115g fresh baby corn, halved lengthways
150g sugar snap peas, trimmed
⅓ cup (45g) roasted slivered almonds
1 tablespoon fish sauce
1 tablespoon sweet chilli sauce

1 Cook rice in large saucepan of boiling water,
uncovered, until just tender; drain. Cover to
keep warm.
2 Meanwhile, heat half the oil in wok; stir-fry
chicken, in batches, until browned. Remove
from wok.
3 Heat remaining oil in wok; stir-fry onion and

chicken singapore noodles

plum chicken with cashews

PLUM CHICKEN WITH CASHEWS

prep + cook time 35 minutes serves 4
nutritional count per serving 18.4g total fat
(3.6g saturated fat); 1814kJ (434 cal);
25.4g carbohydrate; 39.6g protein; 4.6g fibre

2 tablespoons peanut oil
600g chicken breast fillets, sliced thinly
1 medium brown onion (150g), sliced thinly
2 cloves garlic, sliced thinly
1 medium red capsicum (200g), sliced thinly
1 medium yellow capsicum (200g),
    sliced thinly
1 medium carrot (120g), cut into matchsticks
115g baby corn, halved lengthways
⅓ cup (80ml) plum sauce
2 tablespoons japanese soy sauce
⅓ cup (50g) roasted unsalted cashews
⅓ cup firmly packed fresh coriander leaves

1 Heat half the oil in wok; stir-fry chicken, in batches, until browned. Remove from wok.
2 Heat remaining oil in wok; stir-fry onion and garlic until onion softens. Add capsicums, carrot, corn and sauces; stir-fry until vegetables are tender.
3 Return chicken to wok with nuts and coriander; stir-fry until hot, season to taste.
Serve with steamed jasmine rice.

CHICKEN AND SPINACH NOODLES

prep + cook time 25 minutes serves 4
nutritional count per serving 16.1g total fat
(3.5g saturated fat); 1450kJ (347 cal);
19.5g carbohydrate; 28.8g protein; 4g fibre

500g chicken thigh fillets, sliced thinly
¼ cup (60ml) japanese soy sauce
4cm piece fresh ginger (20g), grated
2 cloves garlic, crushed
300g dried rice stick noodles
2 tablespoons peanut oil
200g green beans, trimmed,
    chopped coarsely
150g button mushrooms, sliced thinly
¼ cup (60ml) water
2 teaspoons shrimp paste
300g spinach, trimmed, chopped coarsely

chicken and spinach noodles

1 Combine chicken, sauce, ginger and garlic in medium bowl.
2 Place noodles in large heatproof bowl, cover with boiling water; stand until tender, drain.
3 Heat half the oil in wok; stir-fry chicken, in batches, until browned. Remove from wok.
4 Heat remaining oil in wok; stir-fry beans and mushrooms until tender. Return chicken to wok with noodles, the water and paste; stir-fry until hot. Add spinach; stir-fry until spinach wilts, season to taste.
note Chicken mixture can be marinated for a few hours or overnight.

honey chicken with buk choy and sesame

batches, until browned. Remove from wok.
3 Heat sesame oil in wok; stir-fry onion and
capsicum until vegetables are tender. Add
buk choy and reserved marinade; stir-fry until
mixture boils and buk choy wilts.
4 Return chicken to wok; stir-fry until hot,
season to taste. Serve sprinkled with black
sesame seeds.
Serve with steamed jasmine rice.
note Chicken mixture can be marinated for a few
hours or overnight in the fridge.

CHICKEN AND MUSHROOMS

prep + cook time 35 minutes serves 4
nutritional council per serving 24.3g total fat
(7g saturated fat); 2065kJ (494 cal);
15.9g carbohydrate; 51.1g protein; 4.5g fibre

1 tablespoon peanut oil
1kg chicken thigh fillets, sliced thinly
2 cloves garlic, crushed
8 green onions, chopped coarsely
200g fresh shiitake mushrooms,
    chopped coarsely
200g gai lan, chopped coarsely
100g oyster mushrooms, chopped coarsely
⅓ cup (80ml) vegetarian mushroom oyster
    sauce
100g enoki mushrooms
50g crisp fried noodles

1 Heat oil in wok; stir-fry chicken, in batches,
until browned.
2 Return chicken to wok with garlic and onion;
stir-fry until onion softens. Add shiitake
mushrooms; stir-fry until tender. Add gai lan,
oyster mushrooms and sauce; stir-fry until
vegetables are tender.
3 Remove from heat; toss in enoki mushrooms
and noodles, season to taste.
note Fried noodles are sold in 100g packets in
supermarkets and Asian food stores.

HONEY CHICKEN WITH
BUK CHOY AND SESAME

prep + cook time 30 minutes serves 4
nutritional count per serving 16.2g total fat
(3.6g saturated fat); 1501kJ (359 cal);
22.4g carbohydrate; 30.7g protein; 2.1g fibre

600g chicken thigh fillets, chopped coarsely
¼ cup (60ml) light soy sauce
¼ cup (90g) honey
2cm piece fresh ginger (10g), grated
1 clove garlic, crushed
2 tablespoons finely chopped
    fresh coriander
1 tablespoon finely chopped vietnamese mint
1 tablespoon peanut oil
2 teaspoons sesame oil
1 small red onion (100g), sliced thinly
1 small red capsicum (150g),
    chopped coarsely
300g buk choy, trimmed, shredded finely
2 tablespoons black sesame seeds

1 Combine chicken, sauce, honey, ginger,
garlic and herbs in medium bowl. Drain
chicken; reserve marinade.
2 Heat peanut oil in wok; stir-fry chicken, in

chicken and mushrooms

GINGER AND TERIYAKI CHICKEN

prep + cook time **20 minutes** serves **4**
nutritional count per serving **4.6g total fat**
(1.1g saturated fat); 832kJ (199 cal);
8.1g carbohydrate; 29.8g protein; 2.2g fibre

Cut 2 medium carrots and 1 large red capsicum into matchsticks. Combine 500g thinly sliced chicken breast fillets and 4cm piece grated fresh ginger. Heat oiled wok; stir-fry chicken, in batches, until browned. Remove from wok. Stir-fry carrot and capsicum in wok until tender. Return chicken to wok with 2 tablespoons teriyaki sauce; stir-fry until hot. Season to taste; serve stir-fry sprinkled with ¼ cup loosely packed fresh coriander leaves.
Serve with **steamed jasmine rice.**

HOISIN AND LIME CHICKEN

prep + cook time **15 minutes** serves **4**
nutritional count per serving **2.5g total fat**
(0.4g saturated fat); 548kJ (131 cal);
7.5g carbohydrate; 15.7g protein; 7.5g fibre

Heat ½ teaspoon peanut oil in wok; stir-fry 150g thinly sliced chicken breast fillets until browned. Remove from wok. Stir-fry 1 thinly sliced medium brown onion, 525g coarsely chopped broccolini, 1 thinly sliced fresh long red chilli, 2 thinly sliced garlic cloves and 2 tablespoons of water in wok for 2 minutes. Return chicken to wok with 4 thinly sliced green onions, 2 tablespoons hoisin sauce and 1 tablespoon lime juice; stir-fry until hot, season to taste. Serve with lime wedges.

FAST CHICKEN

HONEY AND MACADAMIA CHICKEN

prep + cook time **25 minutes** serves **4**
nutritional count per serving **29.1g total fat**
(6.2g saturated fat); 2086kJ (499 cal);
13.4g carbohydrate; 45.4g protein; 1.7g fibre

Heat 1 tablespoon peanut oil in wok; stir-fry
800g thinly sliced chicken breast fillets until
browned. Remove from wok. Heat 1 tablespoon
peanut oil in wok; stir-fry 300g coarsely chopped
gai lan until tender. Return chicken to wok with
¼ cup japanese soy sauce and 2 tablespoons
honey; stir-fry until hot, season to taste. Serve
stir-fry sprinkled with ⅓ cup coarsely chopped
roasted macadamias.

CHICKEN AND EGG NOODLES

prep + cook time **20 minutes** serves **4**
nutritional count per serving **12.1g total fat**
(2.6g saturated fat); 1818kJ (435 cal);
49.9g carbohydrate; 30g protein; 3.5g fibre

Place 440g thin egg noodles in large heatproof
bowl, cover with boiling water; separate with
fork, drain. Heat 2 teaspoons vegetable oil in
wok; stir-fry 500g thinly sliced chicken thigh
fillets, in batches, until browned. Remove from
wok. Heat 2 teaspoons vegetable oil in wok;
stir-fry 115g halved baby corn, 120g packet
cantonese sauce and ¼ cup water until corn
is tender. Return chicken to wok with noodles;
stir-fry until hot. Season to taste; serve stir-fry
sprinkled with 2 thinly sliced green onions.

BEEF WITH MIXED MUSHROOMS

prep + cook time 30 minutes serves 4
nutritional count per serving 29.9g total fat
(8.9g saturated fat); 3298kJ (789 cal);
70.1g carbohydrate; 59.2g protein; 6.6g fibre

¼ cup (60ml) peanut oil
800g beef rump steak, sliced thinly
1 medium brown onion (150g), sliced thickly
2 cloves garlic, crushed
2cm piece fresh ginger (10g), grated
2 fresh long red chillies, sliced thinly
150g oyster mushrooms, halved
100g fresh shiitake mushrooms, halved
100g enoki mushrooms
450g hokkien noodles
6 green onions, sliced thickly
¼ cup (60ml) oyster sauce
1 tablespoon kecap manis
1 teaspoon sesame oil

1 Heat half the peanut oil in wok; stir-fry beef, in batches, until browned. Remove from wok.
2 Heat remaining peanut oil in wok; stir-fry onion until softened. Add garlic, ginger, chilli and mushrooms; stir-fry until mushrooms are tender.
3 Meanwhile, place noodles in large heatproof bowl, cover with boiling water; separate with fork, drain.
4 Return beef to wok with noodles and remaining ingredients; stir-fry until hot, season to taste.

BEEF

beef with asparagus and oyster sauce

BEEF CHOW MEIN

prep + cook time **50 minutes** serves **4**
nutritional count per serving **15.7g total fat**
(4.6g saturated fat); 2571kJ (615 cal);
70.6g carbohydrate; 42.3g protein; 8.4g fibre

1 tablespoon vegetable oil
500g beef mince
1 medium brown onion (150g),
 chopped finely
2 cloves garlic, crushed
1 tablespoon curry powder
1 large carrot (180g), chopped finely
2 stalks celery (300g), trimmed, sliced thinly
150g button mushrooms, sliced thinly
1 cup (250ml) chicken stock
⅓ cup (80ml) oyster sauce
2 tablespoons dark soy sauce
440g thin fresh egg noodles
½ cup (60g) frozen peas
½ small wombok (350g), shredded coarsely

1 Heat oil in wok; stir-fry beef, onion and garlic
until beef is browned. Add curry powder;
stir-fry about 1 minute or until fragrant. Add
carrot, celery and mushrooms; stir-fry until
vegetables soften.
2 Add stock, sauces and noodles; stir-fry
2 minutes. Add peas and wombok; stir-fry
until wombok wilts.

BEEF WITH ASPARAGUS AND OYSTER SAUCE

prep + cook time **25 minutes** serves **4**
nutritional count per serving **15.1g total fat**
(3.8g saturated fat); 1166kJ (279 cal);
6.1g carbohydrate; 28.6g protein; 2g fibre

2 tablespoons peanut oil
500g beef rump steak, sliced thinly
1 medium brown onion (150g), cut
 into wedges
340g asparagus, trimmed, cut into
 3cm lengths
2 cloves garlic, chopped finely
2 tablespoons oyster sauce
1 tablespoon japanese soy sauce

1 Heat half the oil in wok; stir-fry beef, in
batches, until browned. Remove from wok.
2 Heat remaining oil in wok; stir-fry onion until
softened. Add asparagus; stir-fry until tender.
3 Return beef to wok with garlic; stir-fry until
fragrant. Add sauces; stir-fry until hot, season
to taste.
Serve with steamed jasmine rice.
note Use broccolini or broccoli instead of the
asparagus, if you like.

beef chow mein

hoisin beef with wombok

HOISIN BEEF WITH WOMBOK

prep + cook time 35 minutes serves 4
nutritional count per serving 22.9g total fat
(5.8g saturated fat); 2082kJ (498 cal);
27.9g carbohydrate; 46g protein; 8.4g fibre

¼ cup (60ml) peanut oil
4 cups (320g) coarsely shredded wombok
½ cup coarsely chopped fresh garlic chives
750g beef strips
1 large red onion (300g), sliced thickly
2 cloves garlic, crushed
1cm piece fresh ginger (5g), grated
1 teaspoon five-spice powder
250g fresh shiitake mushrooms,
    sliced thickly
1 large red capsicum (350g), sliced thinly
½ cup (125ml) hoisin sauce
1 tablespoon soy sauce
1 tablespoon rice wine vinegar

1 Heat 1 tablespoon of the oil in wok; stir-fry
wombok and chives until wombok is wilted.
Remove from wok; cover to keep warm.
2 Heat 1 tablespoon of the remaining oil in
wok; stir-fry beef, in batches, until browned.
Remove from wok.
3 Heat remaining oil in wok; stir-fry onion
until softened. Add garlic, ginger, five-spice,
mushrooms and capsicum; stir-fry until
vegetables are tender. Return beef to wok with
sauces and vinegar; stir-fry until hot, season to
taste. Serve wombok mixture with stir-fry.
note You need half a medium wombok weighing about
500g for this recipe. Wombok is elongated in shape
with pale green, crinkly leaves, and is the most
common cabbage in South-East Asian cooking. It is
found in Asian grocery stores and most supermarkets.

HONEY SESAME BEEF STIR-FRY

prep + cook time 30 minutes serves 4
nutritional count per serving 22g total fat
(4.1g saturated fat); 2596kJ (621 cal);
49.5g carbohydrate; 53.7g protein; 4.8g fibre

450g thin hokkien noodles
1 tablespoon peanut oil
600g beef strips
115g baby corn, halved lengthways

honey sesame beef stir-fry

4 green onions, cut into 4cm lengths
½ cup (70g) roasted unsalted peanuts
2 tablespoons honey
2 tablespoons salt-reduced soy sauce
1 tablespoon oyster sauce
2 tablespoons water
2 teaspoons sesame oil
1 tablespoon toasted sesame seeds

1 Place noodles in large heatproof bowl, cover
with boiling water; separate with fork, drain.
2 Heat half the peanut oil in wok; stir-fry beef,
in batches, until browned. Remove from wok.
3 Heat remaining peanut oil in wok; stir-fry
corn and onion until corn is tender. Return beef
to wok with noodles, nuts and combined
honey, sauces, the water and sesame oil;
stir-fry until hot, season to taste.
4 Serve noodles sprinkled with sesame seeds.
note Hokkien noodles, also known as stir-fry noodles,
are fresh wheat noodles resembling thick, yellow-brown
spaghetti. They are available from most supermarkets.

ginger teriyaki beef

NUTTY BEEF WITH BROCCOLINI

prep + cook time **30 minutes** serves **4**
nutritional count per serving **31.5g total fat
(6.7g saturated fat); 2052kJ (491 cal);
4.2g carbohydrate; 43.8g protein; 5.3g fibre**

600g beef scotch fillet steak, sliced thinly
2 tablespoons dukkah
½ cup (65g) finely chopped roasted
 unsalted pistachios
2 tablespoons peanut oil
2 teaspoons sesame oil
2 shallots (50g), sliced thinly
350g broccolini, chopped coarsely
2 tablespoons kecap manis
2 tablespoons chinese cooking wine

1 Combine beef, dukkah and half the nuts
in medium bowl.
2 Heat half the peanut oil in wok; stir-fry beef,
in batches, until browned. Remove from wok.
3 Heat remaining peanut oil and sesame oil
in wok; stir-fry shallots and broccolini until
broccolini is tender. Return beef to wok with
kecap manis and cooking wine; stir-fry until
hot, season to taste. Serve sprinkled with
remaining nuts.

notes After stir-frying beef, wipe out the wok with
absorbent paper to prevent any remaining spices
or nuts from burning and spoiling the stir-fry.
The beef mixture can be marinated for a few hours
or overnight in the fridge.

GINGER TERIYAKI BEEF

prep + cook time **25 minutes** serves **4**
nutritional count per serving **20.7g total fat
(7.2g saturated fat); 2073kJ (496 cal);
23.2g carbohydrate; 48g protein; 10.5g fibre**

⅓ cup (80ml) teriyaki sauce
½ cup (125ml) hoisin sauce
2 tablespoons mirin
1 tablespoon peanut oil
750g beef strips
250g broccoli, cut into florets
250g sugar snap peas, trimmed
115g fresh baby corn, halved lengthways
4cm piece fresh ginger (20g), grated
1½ cups (120g) bean sprouts

1 Combine sauces and mirin in small jug.
2 Heat half the oil in wok; stir-fry beef, in
batches, until browned. Remove from wok.
3 Heat remaining oil in wok; stir-fry broccoli
until almost tender.
4 Return beef to wok with sauce mixture,
peas, corn and ginger. Stir-fry until vegetables
are tender. Remove from heat; season to taste,
sprinkle with sprouts.

nutty beef with broccolini

CHAR SIU LAMB AND NOODLES

prep + cook time **35 minutes** serves **4**
nutritional count per serving **29.2g total fat**
(9.6g saturated fat); 2725kJ (652 cal);
46.6g carbohydrate; 47.1g protein; 8g fibre

2 cloves garlic, crushed
2cm piece fresh ginger (10g), grated
1 tablespoon finely grated orange rind
1 teaspoon sesame oil
750g lamb strips
450g hokkien noodles
2 tablespoons peanut oil
200g sugar snap peas, trimmed
115g baby corn, halved lengthways
2 fresh long red chillies, sliced thinly
⅓ cup (120g) char siu sauce
2 tablespoons water
1 tablespoon rice wine vinegar

1 Combine garlic, ginger, rind, sesame oil and lamb in medium bowl.
2 Place noodles in large heatproof bowl, cover with boiling water; separate with fork, drain.
3 Heat half the peanut oil in wok; stir-fry peas and corn until just tender. Remove from wok.
4 Heat remaining peanut oil in wok; stir-fry lamb, in batches, until browned. Return lamb, peas and corn to wok with noodles, chilli and the combined sauce, the water and vinegar; stir-fry until hot, season to taste.

lamb with broccolini

LAMB WITH BROCCOLINI

prep + cook time **25 minutes** serves 4
nutritional count per serving 14.6g total fat
(3.6g saturated fat); 1404kJ (336 cal);
8g carbohydrate; 39.7g protein; 6.3g fibre

1 tablespoon peanut oil
600g lamb strips
2 teaspoons sesame oil
1 medium red onion (170g), cut into
   thin wedges
2 cloves garlic, crushed
350g broccolini, cut into 3cm lengths
250g sugar snap peas, trimmed
1 tablespoon water
2 tablespoons sweet chilli sauce
1 tablespoon japanese soy sauce

1 Heat peanut oil in wok; stir-fry lamb, in batches, until browned. Remove from wok.
2 Heat sesame oil in wok; stir-fry onion and garlic until onion softens. Add broccolini, peas and the water; stir-fry until vegetables soften.
3 Return lamb to wok with sauces; stir-fry until hot, season to taste.
Serve with **steamed jasmine rice.**

HONEY AND FIVE-SPICE LAMB WITH BUK CHOY

prep + cook time **25 minutes** serves 4
nutritional count per serving 12.2g total fat
(3.3g saturated fat); 1781kJ (426 cal);
40.7g carbohydrate; 36.1g protein; 3.3g fibre

¼ teaspoon five-spice powder
¼ cup (60ml) oyster sauce
2 tablespoons honey
2 tablespoons rice vinegar
2 cloves garlic, crushed
600g lamb fillets, sliced thinly
400g fresh thin rice noodles
1 tablespoon sesame oil
2 fresh long red chillies, sliced thinly
2cm piece fresh ginger (10g), cut into
   matchsticks
1 medium red onion (150g), sliced thickly
500g baby buk choy, leaves separated

honey and five-spice lamb with buk choy

¼ cup firmly packed fresh coriander leaves
1 tablespoon crushed peanuts

1 Combine five-spice, sauce, honey, vinegar and garlic in small bowl.
2 Combine lamb with 1 tablespoon of the five-spice mixture in medium bowl.
3 Place noodles in large heatproof bowl, cover with boiling water; separate with fork, drain.
4 Heat oil in wok; stir-fry lamb, in batches, until browned. Return lamb to wok, add remaining five-spice mixture, chilli, ginger and onion; stir-fry until onion softens. Add noodles and buk choy; stir-fry until hot, season to taste.
5 Serve stir-fry sprinkled with coriander and nuts.
note Fresh rice noodles are soft white noodles made from rice flour and vegetable oil; they are available in varying thicknesses, from vermicelli-thin to broad and flat. Rinse them under hot water to remove starch and excess oil before using. Available from Asian grocery stores and most supermarkets.

hoisin lamb

MONGOLIAN LAMB AND NOODLES

prep + cook time **40 minutes** serves **4**
nutritional count per serving **17.4g total fat**
(4.5g saturated fat); 2600kJ (622 cal);
63.6g carbohydrate; 44.5g protein; 5.4g fibre

600g lamb backstrap, sliced thinly
⅓ cup (80ml) sweet sherry
2 tablespoons dark soy sauce
2 tablespoons sweet chilli sauce
2 tablespoons peanut oil
1 large brown onion (200g), sliced thinly
2 cloves garlic, crushed
1 medium green capsicum (200g),
    sliced thinly
175g broccolini, cut into 3cm lengths
1 tablespoon brown sugar
1 teaspoon sesame oil
⅓ cup (80ml) chicken stock
400g hokkien noodles

1 Combine lamb with half the sherry, half the soy sauce and half the sweet chilli sauce in medium bowl.
2 Heat half the peanut oil in wok; stir-fry lamb, in batches, until browned. Remove from wok.
3 Heat remaining peanut oil in wok; stir-fry onion and garlic until onion softens. Add capsicum and broccolini; stir-fry until vegetables are tender.
4 Return lamb to wok with remaining ingredients; stir-fry until hot, season to taste.
note Use baby buk choy or gai lan in place of the broccolini. Broccolini is a cross between broccoli and chinese kale; it is milder and sweeter than broccoli. Each long stem is topped by a loose floret that closely resembles broccoli; from floret to stem, broccolini is completely edible.

HOISIN LAMB

prep + cook time **25 minutes** serves **4**
nutritional count per serving **17.2g total fat**
(6.1g saturated fat); 1505kJ (360 cal);
13.8g carbohydrate; 34.5g protein; 6.6g fibre

1 tablespoon peanut oil
1 large brown onion (200g), chopped finely
2 cloves garlic, crushed
5cm piece fresh ginger (25g), grated
1 fresh long red chilli, chopped finely
600g lamb mince
¼ cup (60ml) hoisin sauce
2 tablespoons lime juice
227g can water chestnut slices, rinsed,
    drained, chopped finely
250g (3 cups) bean sprouts
1 cup loosely packed fresh mint leaves
8 large iceberg lettuce leaves

1 Heat oil in wok; stir-fry onion, garlic, ginger and chilli until onion softens. Add mince; stir-fry until browned. Add sauce, juice, chestnuts, sprouts and half the mint; stir-fry until hot, season to taste.
2 Divide lamb mixture between lettuce leaves; sprinkle with remaining mint.

mongolian lamb and noodles

THAI GREEN PORK

prep + cook time 35 minutes serves 4
nutritional count per serving 28.9g total fat
(14.9g saturated fat); 1940kJ (464 cal);
11.4g carbohydrate; 37.7g protein; 5g fibre

2 tablespoons peanut oil
600g pork fillet, sliced thinly
2 tablespoons green curry paste
2 baby eggplants (120g), chopped coarsely
1 large zucchini (150g), chopped coarsely
115g baby corn, halved lengthways
270ml can coconut milk
2 fresh kaffir lime leaves, shredded finely
1 tablespoon lime juice
1 tablespoon fish sauce
2 teaspoons brown sugar
⅓ cup loosely packed fresh coriander leaves

1 Heat half the oil in wok; stir-fry pork, in
batches, until browned. Remove from wok.
2 Heat remaining oil in wok; stir-fry curry paste
until fragrant. Add eggplant, zucchini and corn;
stir-fry until vegetables are tender. Add coconut
milk, kaffir lime leaves, juice, sauce and sugar;
stir-fry 2 minutes. Return pork to wok; stir-fry
until hot, season to taste. Serve stir-fry
sprinkled with coriander.
Serve with steamed jasmine rice.

PORK

pork fried rice

garlic until onion softens. Add bacon and pork; stir-fry until bacon is crisp. Add mushrooms, peas and carrot; stir-fry about 3 minutes or until carrot is just tender.

3 Add rice and kecap manis to wok; stir-fry until hot, season to taste. Toss omelette and onion through fried rice just before serving.

note **You need to cook about 1⅓ cups brown rice for this recipe.**

SWEET AND SOY PORK

prep + cook time **20 minutes** serves **4**
nutritional count per serving **12g total fat**
(2.7g saturated fat); 1622kJ (388 cal);
34.6g carbohydrate; 34g protein; 2.2g fibre

450g fresh wide rice noodles
1½ tablespoons peanut oil
500g pork fillet, sliced thinly
300g gai lan, cut into 5cm lengths,
   stems and leaves separated
3 cloves garlic, crushed
2 tablespoons light soy sauce
2 tablespoons dark soy sauce
2 tablespoons brown sugar
1 egg

1 Place noodles in large heatproof bowl, cover with boiling water; separate with fork, drain.
2 Heat 1 tablespoon of the oil in wok; stir-fry pork, in batches, until browned all over. Remove from wok.
3 Heat remaining oil in wok; stir-fry gai lan stems until tender. Add gai lan leaves and garlic; stir-fry until gai lan wilts. Return pork to wok with noodles, sauces and sugar; stir-fry until hot.
4 Make a well in centre of noodles. Add egg; stir-fry egg until egg and noodle mixture are combined, season to taste.

PORK FRIED RICE

prep + cook time **35 minutes** serves **4**
nutritional count per serving **13g total fat**
(3.7g saturated fat); 1726kJ (413 cal);
42.8g carbohydrate; 28.2g protein; 5.2g fibre

3 teaspoons peanut oil
2 eggs, beaten lightly
1 medium brown onion (150g), sliced thinly
1 clove garlic, crushed
2 rindless bacon rashers (130g), sliced thinly
200g pork fillet, sliced thinly
150g button mushrooms, quartered
150g sugar snap peas, trimmed,
   halved crossways
1 medium carrot (120g), chopped finely
3 cups cold cooked brown long-grain rice
   (see note)
2 tablespoons kecap manis
4 green onions, sliced thinly

1 Heat 1 teaspoon of the oil in wok. Pour half the egg into wok; cook omelette, tilting wok, until omelette is set. Remove omelette from wok; roll tightly then slice thinly. Repeat using another teaspoon of oil and remaining egg.
2 Heat remaining oil in wok; stir-fry onion and

sticky pork with vegies

STICKY PORK WITH VEGIES

prep + cook time 40 minutes (+ refrigeration) serves 4
nutritional count per serving 33.7g total fat
(8.1g saturated fat); 2366kJ (566 cal);
18.5g carbohydrate; 46.4g protein; 3.8g fibre

1 tablespoon honey
2 tablespoons light soy sauce
2 tablespoons brown sugar
1 teaspoon five-spice powder
1 teaspoon hot chilli powder
3 cloves garlic, crushed
1 teaspoon sesame oil
750g pork neck, cut into 3cm cubes
2 tablespoons peanut oil
½ cup (70g) raw peanuts, chopped coarsely
1 medium carrot (120g), cut into matchsticks
150g snow peas, trimmed, sliced thinly
    lengthways
2 tablespoons orange juice
3 fresh kaffir lime leaves, shredded finely
4 green onions, sliced thinly

1 Combine honey, sauce, sugar, five-spice,
chilli, garlic and sesame oil in large bowl;
add pork, turn to coat in marinade. Cover;
refrigerate 3 hours or overnight.
2 Heat half the peanut oil in wok; stir-fry nuts
until browned. Drain.
3 Heat remaining oil in wok; stir-fry pork, in
batches, until browned. Return pork to wok
with carrot; stir-fry until pork is cooked.
4 Add snow peas, juice and lime leaves; stir-fry
until snow peas are tender. Remove from heat;
toss in onion and nuts, season to taste.

PORK LARB WITH BROCCOLINI

prep + cook time 25 minutes serves 4
nutritional count per serving 23.9g total fat
(6g saturated fat); 2006kJ (480 cal);
25g carbohydrate; 39.5g protein; 5.5g fibre

1 tablespoon peanut oil
2 cloves garlic, crushed
600g pork mince
⅓ cup (90g) grated palm sugar
2 tablespoons fish sauce
4 fresh kaffir lime leaves, shredded finely

pork larb with broccolini

½ cup (40g) fried shallots
⅓ cup (45g) roasted unsalted peanuts
350g broccolini, halved lengthways
1 tablespoon lime juice
1 cup loosely packed fresh coriander leaves
1 fresh long red chilli, sliced thinly
2 tablespoons coarsely chopped roasted
    unsalted peanuts

1 Heat oil in wok; stir-fry garlic and mince
until mince is browned. Remove from wok
with slotted spoon.
2 Add sugar, sauce, lime leaves, shallots and
nuts to wok; bring to the boil. Reduce heat;
simmer, uncovered, 1 minute. Return pork to
wok; cook, uncovered, about 2 minutes or
until larb mixture is slightly dry and sticky.
3 Meanwhile, boil, steam or microwave
broccolini until tender; drain.
4 Stir juice and three-quarters of the coriander
into larb; season to taste. Serve larb tossed
with broccolini; sprinkle with remaining
coriander, chilli and coarsely chopped nuts.
note Fried shallots provide a crunchy finish to food;
they're available from Asian grocery stores. Make your
own by frying thinly sliced peeled shallots until crisp.

SWEET AND SOUR PORK

prep + cook time **40 minutes** serves **4**
nutritional count per serving **20.2g total fat
(3.6g saturated fat); 2717kJ (650 cal);
57.7g carbohydrate; 53.7g protein; 7.5g fibre**

800g pork fillet, sliced thinly
1 tablespoon sweet sherry
½ cup (125ml) light soy sauce
¾ cup (110g) plain flour
vegetable oil, for deep-frying
1 tablespoon vegetable oil, extra
1 medium red onion (170g),
    chopped coarsely
2 cloves garlic, crushed
1 medium red capsicum (200g),
    chopped coarsely
1 medium green capsicum (200g),
    chopped coarsely
1 medium carrot (120g), sliced thinly
500g fresh pineapple, chopped coarsely
150g sugar snap peas, trimmed
⅓ cup (80ml) chicken stock
¼ cup (70g) tomato sauce
¼ cup (60ml) white vinegar
¼ cup (55g) white sugar
½ cup loosely packed fresh coriander leaves

1 Combine pork with sherry and 2 tablespoons of the soy sauce in medium bowl; coat pork in flour, shake off excess.
2 Heat oil in wok; deep-fry pork, in batches, until browned and crisp. Drain on absorbent paper. (Strain oil, save for another use.)
3 Heat extra oil in wok; stir-fry onion and garlic until onion softens. Add capsicums and carrot; stir-fry until vegetables are tender. Return pork to wok with pineapple, peas, remaining soy sauce, stock, tomato sauce, vinegar and sugar; stir-fry until hot. Remove from heat; stir in coriander, season to taste.
Serve with **steamed white rice.**
note You need half a pineapple (900g) to get the amount of fresh pineapple required for this recipe. You can use a small can of drained pineapple, instead.

CRISPY BEEF SANG CHOY BOW

prep + cook time **20 minutes** serves **4**
nutritional count per serving **13.3g total fat**
(4.9g saturated fat); 1158kJ (277 cal);
13.8g carbohydrate; 23.7g protein; 4.5g fibre

Heat oiled wok; stir-fry 2 thinly sliced green
onions until soft. Add 400g beef mince; stir-fry
until browned. Add 1 cup frozen peas and
¼ cup hoisin sauce; stir-fry until hot. Remove
from heat; stir in 100g crisp fried noodles and
another 2 thinly sliced green onions, season
to taste. Divide beef mixture between 8 large
iceberg lettuce leaves.

LAMB WITH SPINACH AND RICE NOODLES

prep + cook time **20 minutes** serves **4**
nutritional count per serving **12.5g total fat**
(3.9g saturated fat); 1396kJ (334 cal);
15.2g carbohydrate; 38.4g protein; 1.7g fibre

Trim and coarsely shred 300g spinach. Place
300g dried rice stick noodles in large heatproof
bowl, cover with boiling water; stand until tender,
drain. Heat oiled wok; stir-fry 500g thinly sliced
lamb fillet, in batches, until browned. Remove
from wok. Reheat wok; stir-fry spinach and
2 crushed garlic cloves until spinach wilts. Return
lamb to wok with noodles, ¼ cup kecap manis
and 1 tablespoon japanese soy sauce; stir-fry
until hot, season to taste.

FAST MEAT

CHAR SIU PORK, CORN AND CHOY SUM

prep + cook time **25 minutes** serves **4**
nutritional count per serving **14g total fat**
(3g saturated fat); 1513kJ (362 cal);
18.4g carbohydrate; 37.5g protein; 5.7g fibre

Heat 1 tablespoon peanut oil in wok; stir-fry
600g thinly sliced pork fillet, in batches, until
browned. Remove from wok. Heat another
tablespoon peanut oil in wok; stir-fry 2 coarsely
chopped medium brown onions and 215g baby
corn until onion softens. Return pork to
wok with 300g coarsely chopped choy sum,
2 tablespoons char siu sauce, 2 teaspoons
light soy sauce and 2 teaspoons lime juice;
stir-fry until hot, season to taste. Sprinkle with
1 thinly sliced fresh long red chilli.

BEEF AND BLACK BEAN STIR-FRY

prep + cook time **20 minutes** serves **4**
nutritional count per serving **20.9g total fat**
(6.3g saturated fat); 1739kJ (416 cal);
14.1g carbohydrate; 41.3g protein; 3.3g fibre

Heat 1 tablespoon peanut oil in wok; stir-fry
700g beef strips, in batches, until browned.
Remove from wok. Heat another tablespoon
peanut oil in wok; stir-fry 1 thinly sliced large
brown onion until soft. Add 1 thinly sliced large
red capsicum to pan; stir-fry 1 minute. Return
beef to wok with 250g coarsely chopped baby
choy sum, ½ cup black bean garlic sauce and
2 tablespoons water; stir-fry until choy sum wilts.
Serve with **steamed jasmine rice.**

CHOY SUM WITH CASHEWS

prep + cook time 15 minutes serves 4
nutritional count per serving 23.6g total fat
(4.1g saturated fat); 1271kJ (304 cal);
10g carbohydrate; 10.4g protein; 6.1g fibre

1 tablespoon peanut oil
1 fresh long red chilli, sliced thinly
2 cloves garlic, crushed
2cm piece fresh ginger (10g), grated
1kg choy sum, trimmed, cut into 5cm lengths
2 tablespoons fish sauce
2 tablespoons lime juice
1 cup (150g) roasted unsalted cashews

1 Heat oil in wok; stir-fry chilli, garlic and ginger
1 minute.
2 Add choy sum to wok; stir-fry until almost
tender. Add sauce and juice; stir-fry until hot,
season to taste. Serve sprinkled with nuts.

VEGETABLES

vegetable and omelette fried rice

VEGETABLE AND OMELETTE FRIED RICE

prep + cook time **45 minutes** serves **4**
nutritional count per serving 15.2g total fat
(2.9g saturated fat); 1697kJ (406 cal);
50.6g carbohydrate; 13.3g protein; 6.2g fibre

1 tablespoon peanut oil
2 eggs, beaten lightly
1 medium brown onion (150g), sliced thickly
2 cloves garlic, crushed
3cm piece fresh ginger (15g), grated
1 fresh long red chilli, sliced thinly
1 medium red capsicum (200g), sliced thinly
1 medium carrot (120g), sliced thinly
100g green beans, trimmed,
    chopped coarsely
100g fresh shiitake mushrooms, sliced thinly
3 cups cooked white long-grain rice
    (see note)
2 tablespoons light soy sauce
1 tablespoon oyster sauce
1 teaspoon sesame oil
1 teaspoon five-spice powder
1 cup (80g) bean sprouts
4 green onions, sliced thinly
⅓ cup (50g) roasted unsalted cashews,
    chopped coarsely

1 Heat 1 teaspoon of the oil in wok. Pour half the egg into wok; cook omelette, tilting wok, until omelette is set. Remove omelette from wok; roll tightly then slice thinly. Repeat using another teaspoon of oil and remaining egg.
2 Heat remaining peanut oil in wok; stir-fry brown onion, garlic, ginger and chilli until onion softens. Add capsicum, carrot, beans and mushrooms; stir-fry until vegetables are tender.
3 Add rice, sauces, sesame oil and five-spice; stir-fry until hot. Add sprouts and green onion; stir-fry until heated through, season to taste.
4 Serve fried rice topped with omelette and sprinkled with nuts.

note You need to cook 1½ (300g) white long-grain rice the night before making this recipe. Spread it evenly onto a tray and refrigerate overnight.

hoisin tofu with cashews

HOISIN TOFU WITH CASHEWS

prep + cook time **15 minutes** serves **4**
nutritional count per serving 22.6g total fat
(3.4g saturated fat); 1563kJ (374 cal);
20.9g carbohydrate; 18.2g protein; 8.4g fibre

1 tablespoon vegetable oil
1 fresh long red chilli, sliced thinly
500g packaged fresh stir-fry vegetables
400g packaged marinated tofu pieces,
    chopped coarsely
½ cup (75g) roasted unsalted cashews
⅓ cup (80ml) hoisin sauce
1 tablespoon lime juice

1 Heat oil in wok; stir-fry chilli, vegetables, tofu and nuts until vegetables are just tender.
2 Add sauce and juice; stir-fry until hot, season to taste.

notes We used cryovac-packed ready-to-serve sweet chilli tofu, available from many supermarkets and Asian food stores. Packaged fresh stir-fry vegies are available from supermarkets.

five-spice tofu and noodles
with lemon chilli sauce

4 Heat half the oil in wok; stir-fry tofu, in batches, until browned. Remove from wok.
5 Heat remaining oil in wok; stir-fry onion, garlic and capsicum until onion softens. Add noodles, peas and half the lemon chilli sauce; stir-fry until peas are tender.
6 Serve noodles topped with tofu; drizzle with remaining lemon chilli sauce.

TOFU SANG CHOY BOW

prep + cook time **40 minutes (+ standing)** serves **4**
nutritional count per serving **28g total fat**
(4.5g saturated fat); 1814kJ (434 cal);
12.1g carbohydrate; 30.5g protein; 7.5g fibre

**900g firm silken tofu
peanut oil, for deep-frying
¼ cup (60ml) lemon juice
1 tablespoon grated palm sugar
1½ tablespoons dark soy sauce
1½ teaspoons sambal oelek
1 medium red onion (170g), sliced thinly
2 lebanese cucumbers (260g), seeded, sliced thinly
1 cup (80g) bean sprouts
¼ cup firmly packed thai basil leaves
½ cup firmly packed fresh coriander leaves
8 large iceberg lettuce leaves**

1 Pat tofu dry with absorbent paper; cut into 1.5cm cubes. Spread tofu, in single layer, on absorbent-paper-lined tray; cover tofu with more absorbent paper. Stand 1 hour, changing paper after 30 minutes.
2 Heat oil in wok; deep-fry tofu, in batches, until browned lightly. Drain on absorbent paper.
3 Combine juice, sugar, sauce and sambal in small jug; stir until sugar dissolves.
4 Combine tofu in large bowl with onion, cucumber, sprouts, herbs and dressing, season to taste.
5 Divide mixture among lettuce leaves to serve.

FIVE-SPICE TOFU AND NOODLES WITH LEMON CHILLI SAUCE

prep + cook time **40 minutes** serves **4**
nutritional count per serving **12.2g total fat**
(1.8g saturated fat); 2241kJ (536 cal);
80.3g carbohydrate; 24.6g protein; 8.5g fibre

**½ cup (125ml) sweet chilli sauce
2 teaspoons finely grated lemon rind
¼ cup (60ml) lemon juice
440g fresh egg noodles
⅓ cup (50g) plain flour
2 teaspoons five-spice powder
300g firm tofu, cut into 2cm pieces
1 tablespoon olive oil
1 large brown onion (200g), chopped coarsely
3 cloves garlic, sliced thinly
1 small yellow capsicum (150g), sliced thinly
300g sugar snap peas, trimmed**

1 Combine sauce, rind and juice in small saucepan; bring to the boil. Remove from heat, season to taste.
2 Place noodles in large heatproof bowl, cover with boiling water; separate with fork, drain.
3 Combine flour and five-spice in medium bowl, add tofu; toss to coat in mixture.

tofu sang choy bow

vegetables in oyster sauce

VEGETABLES IN OYSTER SAUCE

prep + cook time 30 minutes serves 4
nutritional count per serving 5.5g total fat
(0.9g saturated fat); 506kJ (121 cal);
9.2g carbohydrate; 5.7g protein; 6.4g fibre

1 tablespoon peanut oil
1 large brown onion (200g), sliced thinly
2 cloves garlic, crushed
450g baby buk choy, quartered lengthways
150g oyster mushrooms, halved
100g enoki mushrooms, trimmed
150g snow peas, trimmed
2 tablespoons vegetarian oyster sauce
1 fresh long red chilli, sliced thinly
¼ cup (20g) fried shallots

1 Heat oil in wok; stir-fry onion and garlic, until
onion softens. Add buk choy, mushrooms and
snow peas; stir-fry until vegetables are tender.
Add sauce; stir-fry until hot, season to taste.
2 Serve stir-fry sprinkled with chilli and shallots;
accompany with lime.

Serve with lime or lemon wedges.

note Vegetarian oyster sauce, based on mushroom
extract and soya beans, has a flavour similar to oyster
sauce and is often used in Asian stir-fries. Use it instead
of oyster sauce in vegetarian dishes.

NOODLES AND BUK CHOY WITH MIXED GARLIC MUSHROOMS

prep + cook time 30 minutes serves 4
nutritional count per serving 11.5g total fat
(2g saturated fat); 1033kJ (247 cal);
84.5g carbohydrate; 20.3g protein; 9.2g fibre

600g fresh thin egg noodles
2 tablespoons peanut oil
1 tablespoon finely grated lemon rind
1 teaspoon dried chilli flakes
2 baby buk choy (300g), leaves separated
¼ cup (60ml) lemon juice
4 cloves garlic, crushed
150g oyster mushrooms, halved
100g fresh shiitake mushrooms, halved
200g swiss brown mushrooms, halved
2 tablespoons kecap manis

noodles and buk choy with
mixed garlic mushrooms

1 Place noodles in large heatproof bowl, cover
with boiling water; separate with fork, drain.
2 Heat half the oil in wok; stir-fry rind and chilli
until fragrant. Add noodles, buk choy and juice;
stir-fry until buk choy wilts. Remove from wok;
cover to keep warm.
3 Heat remaining oil in wok; stir-fry garlic until
fragrant. Add mushrooms and kecap manis;
stir-fry until mushrooms soften, season to taste.
4 Serve mushrooms on noodles.

note When fresh, shiitake mushrooms are also known
as chinese black, forest or golden oak mushrooms.
Although cultivated, they have the earthiness and
taste of wild mushrooms; they are large and meaty
and are often used as a substitute for meat in some
Asian vegetarian dishes.

sweet soy fried noodles

SALT AND PEPPER TOFU

prep + cook time **35 minutes (+ standing)** serves **4**
nutritional count per serving **28.2g total fat**
(4.7g saturated fat); 1772kJ (424 cal);
17.8g carbohydrate; 22g protein; 6.1g fibre

2 x 300g packets firm tofu
1 small red capsicum (150g), sliced thinly
1 small yellow capsicum (150g), sliced thinly
100g snow peas, trimmed, sliced thinly
1 small carrot (70g), sliced thinly
1 cup (80g) bean sprouts
½ cup loosely packed fresh coriander leaves
1 teaspoon coarsely ground black pepper
1 tablespoon sea salt
¼ teaspoon five-spice powder
⅓ cup (50g) plain flour
peanut oil, for deep-frying
chilli lime dressing
2 tablespoons peanut oil
¼ cup (60ml) lime juice
2 tablespoons sweet chilli sauce

1 Dry tofu with absorbent paper. Cut each
piece in half horizontally; cut each half into
quarters (you will have16 pieces). Place tofu
pieces, in single layer, on absorbent paper.
Cover with more absorbent paper; stand
15 minutes.
2 Meanwhile, combine capsicums, snow peas,
carrot, sprouts and coriander in large bowl.
3 Make chilli lime dressing.
4 Combine pepper, salt, five-spice and flour
in medium bowl; coat tofu in flour mixture,
shake away excess. Heat oil in wok; deep-fry
tofu, in batches, until browned lightly. Drain on
absorbent paper.
5 Serve tofu on salad; drizzle with dressing.
chilli lime dressing Whisk ingredients in
small bowl; season to taste.

SWEET SOY FRIED NOODLES

prep + cook time **35 minutes** serves **4**
nutritional count per serving **18.2g total fat**
(4g saturated fat); 2036kJ (487 cal);
55.4g carbohydrate; 20.1g protein; 9.8g fibre

450g fresh wide rice noodles
1 tablespoon peanut oil
3 cloves garlic, sliced thinly
2 eggs, beaten lightly
280g gai lan, chopped coarsely
200g snake beans, trimmed, cut into
    5cm lengths
⅓ cup (80ml) kecap manis
2 tablespoons light soy sauce
½ teaspoon dried chilli flakes
350g packet fried tofu, cut into 2cm pieces
4 green onions, sliced thinly
¾ cup loosely packed thai basil leaves

1 Place noodles in large heatproof bowl, cover
with boiling water; separate with fork, drain.
2 Heat oil in wok; stir-fry garlic until fragrant.
Add egg; stir-fry until set. Add vegetables,
sauces and chilli; stir-fry until vegetables are
tender. Add noodles, tofu, onion and basil;
stir-fry until hot, season to taste.

salt and pepper tofu

coconut rice with capsicum and coriander

COCONUT RICE WITH CAPSICUM AND CORIANDER

prep + cook time **35 minutes** serves **4**
nutritional count per serving **26.2g total fat**
(13.9g saturated fat); 2282kJ (546 cal);
66.4g carbohydrate; 9g protein; 4.5g fibre

½ cup (40g) shredded coconut
2 tablespoons vegetable oil
2 teaspoons chilli oil
1 medium brown onion (150g),
    chopped coarsely
1 medium red capsicum (200g),
    chopped coarsely
3 cloves garlic, crushed
3cm piece fresh ginger (15g), grated
1½ cups (300g) white medium-grain rice
1½ cups (375ml) chicken stock
1 cup (250ml) water
140ml can coconut milk
3 green onions, chopped coarsely
¼ cup coarsely chopped fresh coriander
¼ cup (60ml) lemon juice
¼ cup firmly packed fresh coriander leaves

1 Heat wok; add coconut, stir constantly until browned lightly. Remove from wok.
2 Heat oils in wok; stir-fry brown onion, capsicum, garlic and ginger until onion softens.
3 Add rice; stir-fry 2 minutes. Add stock, the water and coconut milk; simmer, covered, about 20 minutes or until liquid is absorbed and rice is tender.
4 Remove from heat; stir in green onion, chopped coriander, juice and half the coconut, season to taste. Sprinkle with remaining coconut and coriander leaves.

ASIAN GREENS IN BLACK BEAN SAUCE

prep + cook time **25 minutes** serves **4**
nutritional count per serving **13.3g total fat**
(2.6g saturated fat); 2274kJ (544 cal);
89.5g carbohydrate; 15.4g protein; 8.8g fibre

2 cups (400g) jasmine rice
1 tablespoon peanut oil
150g sugar snap peas, trimmed

asian greens in black bean sauce

400g gai lan, chopped coarsely
200g snake beans, trimmed, cut into
    5cm lengths
2 cloves garlic, sliced thinly
1 fresh small red thai chilli, chopped finely
2 medium zucchini (240g), sliced thickly
2 tablespoons black bean sauce
1 tablespoon kecap manis
1 teaspoon sesame oil
⅓ cup (50g) toasted unsalted cashews,
    chopped coarsely

1 Cook rice in large saucepan of boiling water, uncovered, until just tender; drain.
2 Meanwhile, heat peanut oil in wok; stir-fry peas, gai lan stems, beans, garlic, chilli and zucchini until stems are tender.
3 Add sauces, sesame oil, gai lan leaves and nuts; stir-fry until leaves wilt, season to taste.
4 Serve stir-fry with rice.

VEGETARIAN NASI GORENG

prep + cook time **35 minutes** serves **4**
nutritional count per serving **11.2g total fat**
(2.5g saturated fat); 1843kJ (441 cal);
66.8g carbohydrate; 17.6g protein; 7.2g fibre

1 small brown onion (80g), chopped coarsely
2 cloves garlic, quartered
5cm piece fresh ginger (25g),
    chopped coarsely
2 fresh long red chillies, chopped coarsely
1 tablespoon peanut oil
4 eggs, beaten lightly
150g oyster mushrooms, chopped coarsely
1 medium green capsicum (200g),
    chopped coarsely
1 medium red capsicum (200g),
    chopped coarsely
200g fresh baby corn, chopped coarsely
4 cups cold cooked white long-grain rice
    (see note)
1 cup (80g) bean sprouts
3 green onions, sliced thinly
2 tablespoons japanese soy sauce
1 tablespoon kecap manis

1 Blend or process brown onion, garlic, ginger
and chilli until almost smooth.
2 Heat 1 teaspoon of the oil in wok. Pour half
the egg into wok; cook omelette, tilting wok,
until omelette is set. Remove omelette from
wok; roll tightly then slice thickly. Repeat using
another teaspoon of oil and remaining egg.
3 Heat remaining oil in wok; stir-fry brown
onion mixture until fragrant. Add mushrooms,
capsicums and corn; stir-fry until tender.
4 Add rice, sprouts, green onion and sauces;
stir-fry until hot, season to taste.
5 Serve nasi goreng topped with omelette.
note You need to cook about 2 cups white long-grain
rice the night before making this recipe. Spread it evenly
onto a tray and refrigerate overnight.

sweet and sour vegetables with fried tofu

SWEET AND SOUR VEGETABLES WITH FRIED TOFU

prep + cook time **20 minutes** serves **4**
nutritional count per serving **19.9g total fat**
(3.6g saturated fat); 2354kJ (563 cal);
79.6g carbohydrate; 13.8g protein; 8.5g fibre

1 tablespoon peanut oil
1 medium red onion (170g), sliced thinly
1 fresh long red chilli, sliced thinly
250g button mushrooms, quartered
575g jar sweet and sour sauce
200g packet fried tofu, cut into 2cm pieces
150g snow peas, trimmed
115g fresh baby corn, halved lengthways
230g can sliced bamboo shoots,
    rinsed, drained
½ cup (75g) roasted unsalted cashews

1 Heat oil in wok; stir-fry onion, chilli and
mushrooms until onion softens.
2 Add sauce; bring to the boil. Add tofu, peas,
corn and bamboo shoots; stir-fry until hot,
season to taste. Remove from heat; sprinkle
with nuts.
note Packaged fried tofu is available from most
supermarkets.

vegetarian nasi goreng

TOFU PAD THAI

prep + cook time **15 minutes** serves **4**
nutritional count per serving **8.9g total fat**
(1.3g saturated fat); 849kJ (203 cal);
16.2g carbohydrate; 10.9g protein; 7.1g fibre

Place 250g dried rice stick noodles in large
heatproof bowl, cover with boiling water; stand
until tender, drain. Meanwhile, cut 300g firm
tofu into 2cm pieces. Cut 4 green onions into
4cm lengths. Heat oiled wok; stir-fry tofu, in
batches, until browned. Remove from wok.
Reheat wok; stir-fry onion and 2 teaspoons
grated fresh ginger until onion softens. Return
tofu to wok with noodles, 2 tablespoons pad
thai sauce and 2 tablespoons lime juice; stir-fry
until hot, season to taste.

SWEET AND SOUR VEGETABLES

prep + cook time **15 minutes** serves **4**
nutritional count per serving **5.4g total fat**
(0.9g saturated fat); 890kJ (213 cal);
31.8g carbohydrate; 5.2g protein; 8.8g fibre

Heat 1 tablespoon peanut oil in wok; stir-fry
800g packaged traditional stir-fry vegetables
and 115g coarsely chopped baby corn until
vegetables are tender. Add 225g can drained
pineapple pieces, ½ cup sweet and sour sauce
and 50g enoki mushrooms; stir-fry until hot,
season to taste.

SPICED PUMPKIN AND CHICKPEAS

prep + cook time **15 minutes** serves **4**
nutritional count per serving **11g total fat**
(2.1g saturated fat); 828kJ (198 cal);
15.5g carbohydrate; 7.2g protein; 5.4g fibre

Cut 500g pumpkin into 1cm pieces. Heat
2 tablespoons peanut oil in wok; stir-fry
pumpkin about 6 minutes or until almost
tender. Add 1 tablespoon chermoula spice
mix; stir-fry about 2 minutes or until pumpkin
is tender. Add rinsed and drained 420g can
chickpeas and 350g coarsely chopped spinach;
stir-fry until spinach wilts, season to taste.
Serve with **steamed jasmine rice and lemon wedges.**

UDON WITH CHILLI MIXED VEGETABLES

prep + cook time **20 minutes** serves **4**
nutritional count per serving **8.1g total fat**
(1.1g saturated fat); 1083kJ (259 cal);
37.4g carbohydrate; 6.5g protein; 4.7g fibre

Place 440g fresh udon noodles in large
heatproof bowl, cover with boiling water;
separate with fork, drain. Heat oiled wok;
stir-fry 440g packet traditional stir-fry vegetables,
100g enoki mushrooms and 2 thinly sliced
fresh long red chillies until vegetables wilt. Add
noodles and ¼ cup harissa paste; stir-fry until
hot, season to taste.

CHAR SIU VEGETABLES

prep + cook time **15 minutes** serves **4**
nutritional count per serving **7.3g total fat**
(1.1g saturated fat); 568kJ (136 cal);
10.3g carbohydrate; 4.4g protein; 6.8g fibre

Heat 1 tablespoon peanut oil in wok; stir-fry
1 thinly sliced medium red onion until soft. Add
350g coarsely chopped gai lan, 300g coarsely
chopped choy sum and ¼ cup char siu sauce;
stir-fry until greens wilt, season to taste.
Sprinkle vegetables with 1 tablespoon toasted
sesame seeds.
Serve with **steamed jasmine rice.**

HONEY AND GINGER PORK

prep + cook time **20 minutes** serves **4**
nutritional count per serving **10.5g total fat**
(2.2g saturated fat); 1300kJ (311 cal);
16g carbohydrate; 35.1g protein; 1.6g fibre

Combine 2 tablespoons each japanese soy
sauce, mirin and honey in small jug with ¼ cup
water, 2 teaspoons sesame oil, 2 crushed
garlic cloves and 4cm piece grated fresh
ginger. Meanwhile, heat 1 tablespoon sesame
oil in wok; stir-fry 600g thinly sliced pork fillets,
in batches, until browned. Remove from wok.
Stir-fry 1 thinly sliced small red onion and 150g
trimmed sugar snap peas until tender. Return
pork to wok with sauce mixture; stir-fry until
hot, season to taste.
Serve with **hot hokkien noodles.**

LAMB WITH MIXED PEAS

prep + cook time **35 minutes** serves **4**
nutritional count per serving **19.6g total fat**
(4.9g saturated fat); 1517kJ (363 cal);
7.9g carbohydrate; 36.8g protein; 4.6g fibre

Combine 600g thickly sliced lamb fillets,
1 tablespoon kecap manis and 2 tablespoons
each of rice vinegar, peanut oil and char siu
sauce in medium bowl. Drain lamb; reserve
sauce mixture. Cook lamb, in batches, in
heated oiled wok until browned. Return lamb to
wok with reserved sauce mixture, 200g trimmed
snow peas and 200g sugar snap peas; stir-fry
until mixture boils, season to taste. Sprinkle
with 1 thinly sliced fresh long red chilli.

PLUM AND SOY WOK-FRIED PORK

prep + cook time **20 minutes** serves **4**
nutritional count per serving **13.2g total fat**
(2.9g saturated fat); 1668kJ (399 cal);
30.4g carbohydrate; 37.7g protein; 3.3g fibre

Heat 1 tablespoon peanut oil in wok; stir-fry
600g thinly sliced pork fillets, in batches, until
browned. Remove from wok. Heat another
tablespoon peanut oil in wok; stir-fry 1 thickly
sliced large brown onion and 1 crushed garlic
clove for 1 minute. Add 340g trimmed asparagus
and 2 thinly sliced medium red capsicums;
stir-fry until softened. Return pork to wok with
combined ½ cup plum sauce and 2 tablespoons
light soy sauce; stir-fry until hot, season to taste.
Serve with **steamed jasmine rice.**

SHORT ORDER STIR-FRIES

TERIYAKI BEEF NOODLES

prep + cook time **20 minutes** serves **4**
nutritional count per serving **18.9g total fat**
(5.5g saturated fat); 2245kJ (537 cal);
47.8g carbohydrate; 41.5g protein; 3.8g fibre

Cook 270g dried soba noodles in large saucepan
of boiling water, uncovered, until tender; drain.
Meanwhile, heat 2 tablespoons peanut oil in
wok; stir-fry 600g thinly sliced beef eye-fillet, in
batches, until browned. Return beef to wok.
Cut 6 green onions into 5cm lengths, add to
wok; stir-fry until soft. Add ⅓ cup teriyaki sauce
and noodles to wok; stir-fry until hot. Remove
from heat; stir in 2 cups bean sprouts, season
to taste.

FRIED RICE WITH TOMATO, PINEAPPLE AND SNOW PEAS

prep + cook time **20 minutes** serves **4**
nutritional count per serving **5.4g total fat**
(0.8g saturated fat); 1354kJ (324 cal);
57.1g carbohydrate; 8.4g protein; 4.7g fibre

Heat 1 tablespoon peanut oil in wok; stir-fry
200g trimmed and thickly sliced snow peas,
4 thinly sliced green onions and 2 crushed
garlic cloves until peas are tender. Add 4 cups
cold cooked white long-grain rice, ¼ cup
japanese soy sauce, 1 tablespoon fish sauce
and 1 tablespoon lime juice; stir-fry until hot.
Remove from heat; stir in 500g coarsely
chopped fresh pineapple and 2 seeded and
coarsely chopped tomatoes, season to taste.
Serve fried rice sprinkled with ½ cup loosely
packed fresh coriander leaves.

note **You need to cook 2 cups white long-grain rice the**
day before making this recipe. Spread it evenly onto a
tray and refrigerate overnight.

HOISIN AND SWEET CHILLI LAMB

prep + cook time **25 minutes** serves **4**
nutritional count per serving **23.1g total fat**
(8.7g saturated fat); 1877kJ (449 cal);
17.2g carbohydrate; 41.4g protein; 4.5g fibre

Heat 1 tablespoon peanut oil in wok; stir-fry
750g lamb strips, in batches, until browned.
Remove from wok. Heat another tablespoon
peanut oil in wok; stir-fry 2 thinly sliced garlic
cloves and 400g packet stir-fry vegetables until
vegetables are almost tender. Return lamb to
wok with ⅓ cup hoisin sauce, 2 tablespoons
sweet chilli sauce and 2 tablespoons water;
stir-fry until hot, season to taste.

BEEF IN SATAY SAUCE

prep + cook time **30 minutes** serves **4**
nutritional count per serving **42.2g total fat**
(15g saturated fat); 2629kJ (629 cal);
10.6g carbohydrate; 49.8g protein; 6.1g fibre

Heat 1 tablespoon peanut oil in wok; stir-fry
750g beef strips, in batches, until browned.
Remove from wok. Heat another tablespoon
peanut oil in wok; stir-fry 1 thinly sliced fresh
long red chilli, 1 thinly sliced medium brown
onion and 1 thinly sliced medium red capsicum
until soft; remove from wok. Combine ½ cup
peanut butter, ½ cup coconut cream, ¼ cup
sweet chilli sauce and 1 tablespoon japanese
soy sauce in wok; bring to the boil. Return beef
and onion mixture to wok; stir-fry until hot,
season to taste.

ALLSPICE also known as pimento or jamaican pepper; so-named because is tastes like a combination of nutmeg, cumin, clove and cinnamon – all spices.

ASIAN GREENS, BABY a mix of baby buk choy, choy sum, gai lan and water spinach. Don't generally store well due to their high water content so it's best to use them on the day of buying.

BEAN SPROUTS also known as bean shoots; tender new growths of assorted beans and seeds germinated for consumption as sprouts. The most readily available are mung bean, soya bean, alfalfa and snow pea sprouts.

BEANS, SNAKE long (about 40cm), thin, round, fresh green beans, Asian in origin, with a taste similar to green or french beans. Also called yard-long beans because of their (pre-metric) length.

CAJUN SPICE MIX used to give an authentic American Deep South spicy cajun flavour to food; this packaged blend of assorted herbs and spices can include paprika, basil, onion, fennel, thyme, cayenne and tarragon.

CAPSICUM come in many colours: red, green, yellow, orange and purplish-black. Discard seeds and membranes before use.

CHEESE

fetta crumbly goat- or sheep-milk cheese with a sharp salty taste.

haloumi a firm, cream-coloured sheep-milk cheese; a bit like a minty, salty fetta in flavour. Can be grilled or fried, briefly, without breaking down. Should be eaten while still warm as it becomes tough and rubbery on cooling.

parmesan also known as parmigiano, a hard, grainy cows'-milk cheese.

CHERMOULA SPICE MIX a North African spice blend which, when sprinkled onto chicken and lamb before cooking, gives a spicy Moroccan flavour. It is a blend of cumin, paprika, onion, turmeric, cayenne pepper, garlic, parsley, salt and pepper.

CHICKPEAS also called channa, garbanzos or hummus; round, sandy-coloured legume.

CHILLI available in many different types and sizes. Use rubber gloves when seeding and chopping fresh chillies as they can burn your skin. Removing seeds and membranes lessens the heat level.

jam a sweet, sourish tangy jam; sold in jars at supermarkets or Asian food stores.

flakes, dried dehydrated deep-red chilli slices and whole seeds; good for use in cooking or as a condiment for sprinkling over cooked foods.

green usually any unripened chilli, but may include some varieties that are green when ripe.

long red available both fresh and dried; a generic term used for any moderately hot, long (about 6cm-8cm), thin chilli.

red thai small, medium hot, and bright red in colour.

CHINESE BARBECUED DUCK traditionally cooked in special ovens, this duck has a sticky sweet coating made from soy sauce, sherry, five-spice and hoisin sauce. It is available from Asian food stores.

CHINESE BARBECUE PORK also called char siew. Traditionally cooked in special ovens, this pork has a sweet, sticky coating made from soy sauce, sherry, five-spice powder and hoisin sauce. Available from Asian food stores.

CHINESE COOKING WINE made from glutinous rice fermented with water, has a dark straw colour and a unique flavour. It is available in Asian food stores and many larger supermarkets. Substitute with dry sherry.

CHORIZO a sausage of Spanish origin, made of coarsely ground pork and highly seasoned with garlic and chillies.

COCONUT

cream is obtained commercially from the first pressing of the coconut flesh alone, without the addition of water; the second pressing (less rich) is sold as the milk. Available in cans and cartons at supermarkets.

milk the second pressing (less rich) from grated mature coconut flesh; available in cans and cartons.

CORIANDER also known as pak chee, cilantro or chinese parsley; bright-green leafy herb with a pungent flavour. The stems and roots of coriander are also used in cooking; wash well before using. Also available as ground or as seeds; these should not be substituted for fresh coriander as the tastes are completely different.

CORNFLOUR also known as cornstarch; used as a thickening agent. Available as 100% corn (maize) and wheaten cornflour.

GLOSSARY

CRANBERRIES, DRIED they have the same slightly sour, succulent flavour as fresh cranberries. Available in most supermarkets.

CUMIN a spice also known as zeera or comino; has a spicy, nutty flavour.

EGGPLANT purple-skinned vegetable also known as aubergine.

baby also known as finger or japanese eggplant; very small and slender.

FISH FILLETS, FIRM WHITE any boneless firm white fish fillet – ling, bream, swordfish, whiting, blue eye or sea perch are all good choices. Check for any small pieces of bone in the fillets and use tweezers to remove them.

FIVE-SPICE POWDER (also known as chinese five-spice) a fragrant mixture of ground cinnamon, cloves, star anise, sichuan pepper and fennel seeds.

FLOUR

plain an all-purpose flour made from wheat.

self-raising plain flour sifted with baking powder in the proportion of 1 cup flour to 2 teaspoons baking powder.

GINGER also known as green or root ginger; the thick root of a tropical plant.

ground also known as powdered ginger; used as a flavouring in cakes and pies, but cannot be substituted for fresh ginger.

HARISSA a Moroccan sauce or paste made from dried chillies, cumin, garlic, oil and caraway seeds. Available in Middle-Eastern food shops and most major supermarkets.

KECAP MANIS see sauces, soy.

LEMON PEPPER also known as lemon pepper seasoning, a blend of crushed black pepper, lemon, herbs and spices.

MINCE also known as ground meat.

MIRIN is a Japanese champagne-coloured cooking wine; made of glutinous rice and alcohol and used expressly for cooking. Do not be confused with sake.

NASI GORENG SPICE MIX a blend of chilli, garlic, red chilli, sugar, amchur, shrimp powder, galangal and ginger. Available from Asian food stores and the Asian section of larger supermarkets.

NOODLES

crispy fried noodles are sold packaged (commonly a 100g packet), already deep-fried and ready to eat. They are sometimes labelled 'crunchy noodles'.

rice vermicelli also known as sen mee, mei fun or bee hoon. Used throughout Asia in spring rolls and cold salads; similar to bean threads, only longer and made with rice flour instead of mung bean starch. Before using, soak the dried noodles in hot water until softened, boil them briefly then rinse with hot water.

singapore pre-cooked wheat noodles best described as a thinner version of hokkien; sold, packaged, in the refrigerated section of supermarkets.

OIL

olive made from ripened olives. Extra virgin and virgin are the first pressing of the olive and is considered the best, while extra light or light refers to taste not fat levels.

peanut pressed from ground peanuts; most commonly used oil in Asian cooking because of its high smoke point (capacity to handle high heat without burning).

sesame made from roasted, crushed, white sesame seeds.

vegetable sourced from plants rather than animal fats.

ONIONS

green also known as scallion or, incorrectly, shallot; an immature onion picked before the bulb has formed, having a long, bright-green edible stalk.

red also known as red spanish, spanish or bermuda onion; a large, sweet-flavoured, purple-red onion.

purple shallots also known as asian shallots, pink shallots or homm; thin-layered and intensely flavoured, they are available from Asian food shops.

spring an onion with a small white bulb and long narrow green-leafed tops.

PAPRIKA ground dried sweet red capsicum (bell pepper); there are many types available, including sweet, hot, mild and smoked.

PERI PERI (piri piri) a hot spicy Afro-Portuguese chilli paste or powder, is available from major supermarkets and spice stores.

PRAWNS also known as shrimp.

SAMBAL OELEK (also ulek or olek) a salty paste made from chillies and vinegar.

SAUCES

barbecue a spicy, tomato-based sauce used to marinate or baste.

black bean a Chinese sauce made from fermented soya beans, spices, water and wheat flour.

cantonese classic Cantonese sauces are light, mellow and more bland when compared to the thicker, darker and richer sauces of other Chinese cuisines. Spring onion, sugar, salt, rice wine, soy sauce, cornflour, vinegar, sesame oil, and other oils are used to enhance the flavour. Prepared cantonese sauces are available from Asian grocery stores and supermarkets.

pad thai a Thai-style sauce containing an oyster sauce, palm sugar, soy sauce, fish sauce, tamarind and shallots. It has a sweet, salty, spicy flavour.

soy also known as sieu, is made from fermented soya beans. Several variations are available in most supermarkets and Asian food stores. We use Japanese soy unless indicated otherwise; it is possibly the best table soy and the one to choose if you only want one variety.

dark soy is deep brown, almost black in colour; is richer with a thicker consistency than other types. Pungent but not salty.

tamari a thick, dark soy sauce made mainly from soya beans without the wheat used in standard soy sauce.

sweet and sour a blend of tomatoes, onions, capsicum, carrots, pineapple and spices.

tomato pasta a prepared sauce made from a blend of tomatoes, herbs and spices.

worcestershire a dark-coloured condiment made from garlic, soy sauce, tamarind, onions, molasses, lime, anchovies, vinegar and seasonings.

SHIITAKE MUSHROOMS When dried, are known as donko or dried chinese mushrooms; rehydrate before use.

SHRIMP PASTE also known as trasi and blachan; a strong-scented, almost solid preserved paste made of salted dried shrimp. Used as a pungent flavouring in many South-East Asian soups and sauces. Use it sparingly because a little goes a long way.

SNOW PEAS also called mange tout ("eat all").

snow pea sprouts tender new growths of snow peas; also known as mange tout.

SUGAR

brown an extremely soft, finely granulated sugar retaining molasses for its characteristic colour and flavour.

caster also known as superfine or finely granulated table sugar.

palm also known as nam tan pip, jaggery, jawa or gula melaka; made from the sap of the sugar palm tree. Light brown to black in colour and usually sold in rock-hard cakes; the sugar of choice in Indian and most South-East Asian cooking. Substitute it with brown sugar if unavailable.

SUGAR SNAP PEAS also known as honey snap peas; fresh small pea which can be eaten whole, pod and all, just like snow peas.

TAMARI see sauces.

TAMARIND CONCENTRATE the distillation of tamarind pulp into a condensed paste; adds a tart sour taste to dishes. Found in Asian food stores and most major supermarkets.

TOFU also known as bean curd, an off-white, custard-like product made from the "milk" of crushed soya beans; comes fresh as soft or firm. Leftover fresh tofu can be refrigerated in water (which is changed daily) for up to 4 days.

firm made by compressing bean curd to remove most of the water. Good used in stir-fries because it can be tossed without falling apart.

tofu, silken refers to the method by which it is made – where it is strained through silk.

VINEGAR

balsamic made from the juice of Trebbiano grapes; it is a deep rich brown colour with a sweet and sour flavour.

brown malt made from fermented malt and beech shavings.

chinese black a deep, dark vinegar that has a complex, smoky, malty flavour that works well in stir-fries, braises and marinades. It is available from Asian grocery stores and some larger supermarkets.

rice a colourless vinegar made from fermented rice and flavoured with sugar and salt. Also known as seasoned rice vinegar.

white made from the spirit of cane sugar.

WASABI a Japanese horseradish available as a paste in tubes or powdered in tins from Asian food stores and some supermarkets.

WILD RICE BLEND a packaged mixture of white long-grain and dark brown wild rice. The latter is the seed of a North American aquatic grass, which has a distinctively nutty flavour and a crunchy, resilient texture.

CONVERSION CHART

MEASURES

One Australian metric measuring cup holds approximately 250ml, one Australian metric tablespoon holds 20ml, one Australian metric teaspoon holds 5ml.

The difference between one country's measuring cups and another's is within a 2- or 3-teaspoon variance, and will not affect your cooking results. North America, New Zealand and the United Kingdom use a 15ml tablespoon. All cup and spoon measurements are level. The most accurate way of measuring dry ingredients is to weigh them. When measuring liquids, use a clear glass or plastic jug with metric markings.

We use large eggs with an average weight of 60g.

DRY MEASURES

METRIC	IMPERIAL
15g	½oz
30g	1oz
60g	2oz
90g	3oz
125g	4oz (¼lb)
155g	5oz
185g	6oz
220g	7oz
250g	8oz (½lb)
280g	9oz
315g	10oz
345g	11oz
375g	12oz (¾lb)
410g	13oz
440g	14oz
470g	15oz
500g	16oz (1lb)
750g	24oz (1½lb)
1kg	32oz (2lb)

LIQUID MEASURES

METRIC	IMPERIAL
30ml	1 fluid oz
60ml	2 fluid oz
100ml	3 fluid oz
125ml	4 fluid oz
150ml	5 fluid oz (¼ pint)
190ml	6 fluid oz
250ml	8 fluid oz
300ml	10 fluid oz (½ pint)
500ml	16 fluid oz
600ml	20 fluid oz (1 pint)
1000ml (1 litre)	1¾ pints

LENGTH MEASURES

METRIC	IMPERIAL
3mm	⅛in
6mm	¼in
1cm	½in
2cm	¾in
2.5cm	1in
5cm	2in
6cm	2½in
8cm	3in
10cm	4in
13cm	5in
15cm	6in
18cm	7in
20cm	8in
23cm	9in
25cm	10in
28cm	11in
30cm	12in (1ft)

OVEN TEMPERATURES

These oven temperatures are only a guide for conventional ovens.
For fan-forced ovens, check the manufacturer's manual.

	°C (CELSIUS)	°F (FAHRENHEIT)	GAS MARK
Very slow	120	250	½
Slow	150	275-300	1-2
Moderately slow	160	325	3
Moderate	180	350-375	4-5
Moderately hot	200	400	6
Hot	220	425-450	7-8
Very hot	240	475	9

INDEX

If you like this cookbook, you'll love these...

Women's Weekly
after work healthy

Women's Weekly
slow cooked

Women's Weekly
last-minute meals

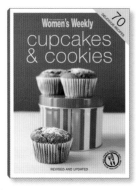

Women's Weekly
cupcakes & cookies

Women's Weekly
easy barbecues

Women's Weekly
simple salads

These are just a small selection of titles available in *The Australian Women's Weekly* range on sale at selected newsagents and supermarkets or online at **www.acpbooks.com.au**